ABC Reading eggs

My First Sight Words

By Sara Leman

Ages 5–7

Dear Parent or Carer,

This book is part of the **My First** series of **Reading Eggs** workbooks. **Reading Eggs** has proven to be very popular with parents, children and teachers. The **Reading Eggs** books and website have helped more than 20 million children worldwide learn to read.

Each vibrant book in the **My First** series includes a wide range of interesting activities that will help your child develop essential reading and writing skills. Written by experienced teachers and educators, the series supports what your child learns at school.

The pages are clear and uncluttered, with activities that build real skills. Activities are fun and motivate children to continue working and learning. Instructions are easy to follow and regular challenges entice children to extend their learning.

I hope that you and your child enjoy using this and other books in the series.

Kind regards, Katy Pike
Publisher

ABC Reading Eggs My Sight Words

ISBN: 978-1-74215-172-4

Reprinted 2011, 2013, 2014, 2015, 2016, 2018, 2019, 2020, 2021, 2022, 2023, 2024, 2025

Distributed by:
Pascal Press
PO Box 250
Glebe NSW 2037

www.readingeggs.com
Written by Sara Leman
Publisher: Katy Pike
Editors: Sandra Iannella and Stacey Weston
Design and layout by Modern Art Production Group
Printed in China by 1010 Printing International Ltd

Contents

Suggestions for Sight Word activities to do at home

- Old magazines and junk mail can be used for a variety of activities including:
  - searching for and circling particular words, such as **only, these, now**
  - cutting out individual letters or sight words to create a collage e.g. **words that begin with 'o'**.

- Allow your child to play with magnetic letters on the fridge to create words. Rearrange the letters to make new words, e.g. **when = we, he, new, hen**.

  Create crosswords, e.g.

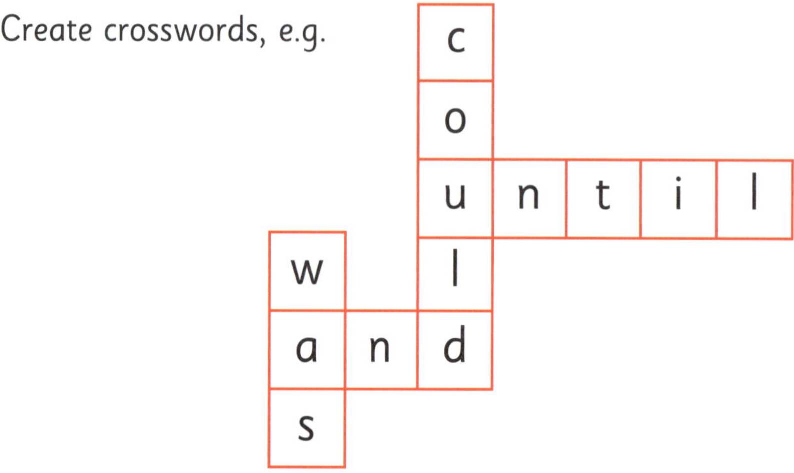

- Encourage your child to write sight words on steamed-up mirrors and windows at home and in the car.

- Trace words on your child's back and ask them to guess what you have written. Alternatively, ask your child to trace words in the air with their finger.

- Allow your child to create words in shaving foam, sand, paint, playdough, string or pavement chalk.

- Play a variation of 'hangman'. Choose a word that the child knows and ask them to fill in the blanks. Alternatively, play 'What am I writing?' Write the first letter of the word and ask your child to guess what the word might be. Then write the second letter and so on until your child guesses correctly or the word is complete.

- Making simple flashcards for your child is a great way to reinforce sight words. Activities to try include:
  - Give me a sentence. Choose 5 sight words and write each word on a card. Ask your child to choose a card and to give you a sentence that uses that sight word. Repeat with the remaining cards.
  - Listen to the sentence. Say a sentence aloud to your child and emphasise the sight word within it. Ask your child to try to locate the sight word from a small selection of flashcards. This activity will help your child to make the association between the spoken and written word.
  - Unscrambling sentences. Make up a simple sentence e.g. **How are you today?** Write each word on a flashcard and shuffle the cards. Lay them out and let your child unscramble the sentence. Point out clues such as a capital letter at the start of the sentence and the punctuation mark at the end.
  - Bingo. Create a 3 × 2 grid for your child and fill it with 6 sight words. Write matching words on flashcards. Select a flashcard, read the word aloud to your child and encourage them to cross off the corresponding word on their grid.

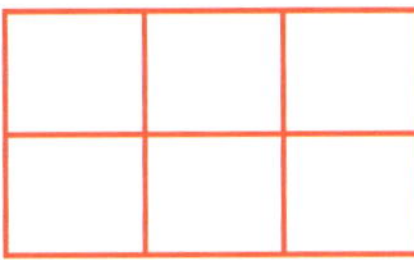

  - Concentration. Choose 6 sight words and write each word on two cards. Shuffle the cards and lay them face down. The child turns over one card at a time and has to try to remember where the matching word is in order to make a pair.
  - Snap. This can be played using the flashcards from the 'concentration' activity. 'Snap' and 'concentration' games help to build your child's visual recognition skills.

- Laminate a plain piece of A4 paper. Use a marker and write one of the tricky sight words, for example **because**. Use the laminated paper as a table placemat for your child. Encourage your child to look at the word and say the word aloud a few times before each meal. Once the word has been committed to memory, wipe it off and write a new one.

- Use the **Reading Eggs Alphabet Flashcards** and the **Reading Eggs Beginning to Read Flashcards** to practise making new words. Activities to try include:

Reading Eggs Alphabet Flashcards
- **Game 7** Making Words

Reading Eggs Beginning to Read Flashcards
- **Game 4** Sight Words
- **Game 5** Make a Sentence

Sight Word chart

List of 96 words covered

so	her	go
we	with	me
the	here	he
to	then	do
as	than	has
and	they	can
but	some	put
how	give	now
see	little	saw
for	which	of
his	could	him
you	said	your
are	about	from
one	all	on
in	because	into
my	also	why

after	no	other
this	be	that
there	she	where
when	too	what
these	was	thing
them	any	their
come	got	done
have	were	leave
better	say	pretty
who	not	while
would	it	should
again	our	pair
out	more	house
shall	only	will
before	until	been
always	by	along

Lesson 1 • so, no, go

1 Trace and copy each word.

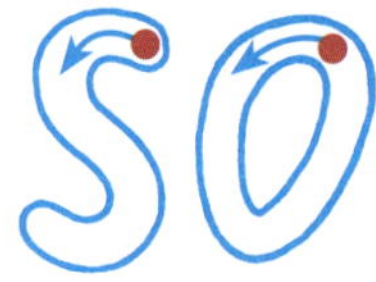

go

2 Colour so = red, colour no = blue, colour go = green.

3 Complete.

s____

____o

g____

4 Guess the word by its shape. Write each word in a box.

so no go

 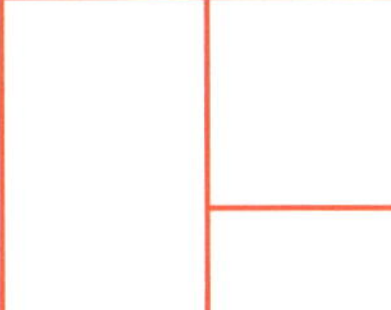 

5 Circle the correct word. Cross out the wrong word.

A green light tells you to go no .

Happy Nap is go so sleepy.

There are no so chips for Charlie Chimp.

You can no go with Sam the Ant.

We were running so go late.

CHALLENGE Circle the hidden words.

a l g o r t s o m n o v t g o v w s o r n o

Lesson 2 • we, me, be

1 **Join each letter to Me Be Fish. Write the words.**

2 **Colour we = red, colour me = blue, colour be = yellow.**

3 **Write the words in alphabetical order.**

4 **Read the clue. Write the word.**

A word that means myself. ________

A word that means us. ________

5 **Complete the sentences.**

me We be

________ can see Issy Me on a flower.

Tom the Dog will ________ here soon.

Meg the Hen gave ________ an egg.

CHALLENGE

Write the word me. Draw a picture of yourself. Write these labels:

head body
arms legs

Lesson 3 • he, the, she

1 Trace and write the words.

2 Match the word to its picture.

he

she

3 Colour the word **the**.

the

the

he

me

be

the

the

the

4 **Help Sid the Kid get to the park.**
Draw a track of he the she words.

5 **Circle the words.**

He She the

Jazz the Cat has a hat. She loves her hat. Sam the Ant has a bag. He wants a new bag.

Colour a star each time you find a word.

CHALLENGE

Write sentences using these words.

he the she

Lesson 4 • to, do, too

1 Help Smile do his washing. Colour the path of to words.

to	to	he	we
if	to	to	of
we	in	to	at
he	is	to	to

2 Trace and write the words.

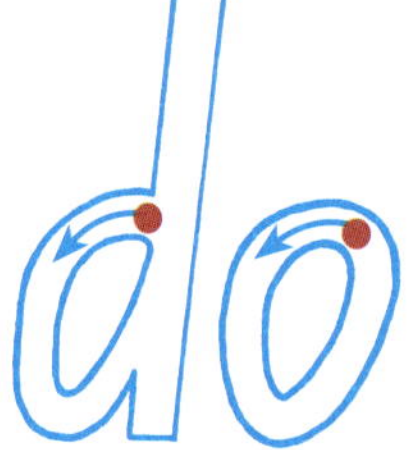

Complete the words.

3 Crack the code!

o = ✿
t = ★
d = ■
n = ✓

1 ★ ✿ ✿ ____________

2 ■ ✿ ____________

3 ★ ✿ ____________

4 ✓ ✿ ____________

5 ✿ ✓ ____________

6 ✓ ✿ ★ ____________

4 Complete the sentences.

to Do too

________ you like Gemma's big bow?

Can I have some cake ________ ?

Give the bone ________ Tom the Dog.

CHALLENGE Write or draw a list of:

"Things I can do".

Lesson 5 • as, has, was

1 Colour as = blue, colour has = green, colour was = red.

2 Join the letters. Write the words.

has was as

______

______

______

3 Guess the word by its shape. Write each word in a box.

as has was

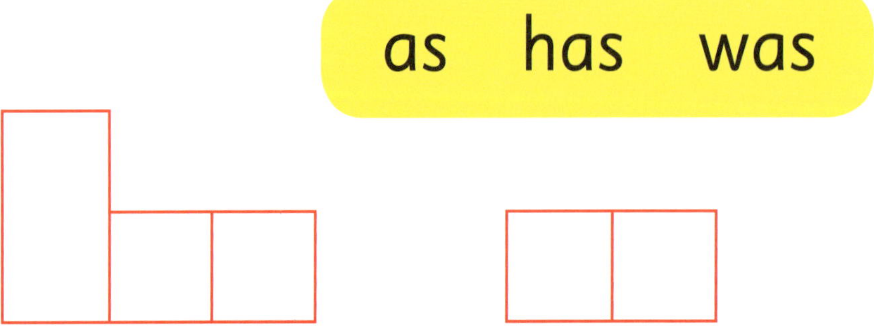

4 Write the words in alphabetical order.

__________ __________ __________

5 Circle the correct word. Cross out the wrong word.

It **was** **has** Dan's birthday.

Yetiyo **has** **as** lots of yoyos.

I can jump **was** **as** far as Kangako.

CHALLENGE

Look for the words

as has was

in an old magazine or newspaper. Cut them out and glue them on paper. Write a sentence for each word.

Lesson 6 • and, can, any

1 **Join Sandy Can to the word can.**

can

no

yes

can

can

can

on

2 **Write and in the middle of each pair.**

burger ________ fries

knife ________ fork

shoes ________ socks

bucket ________ spade

3

Colour yes or no.

Does she have any cups?	yes	no
Does she have any bags?	yes	no
Does she have any dogs?	yes	no
Does she have any hats?	yes	no

4

Join the words that rhyme.

and	man
can	Penny
any	hand

CHALLENGE Write down 5 things that you can do.

I can ____________ .

Lesson 7 • but, put, got

1 Trace and copy each word.

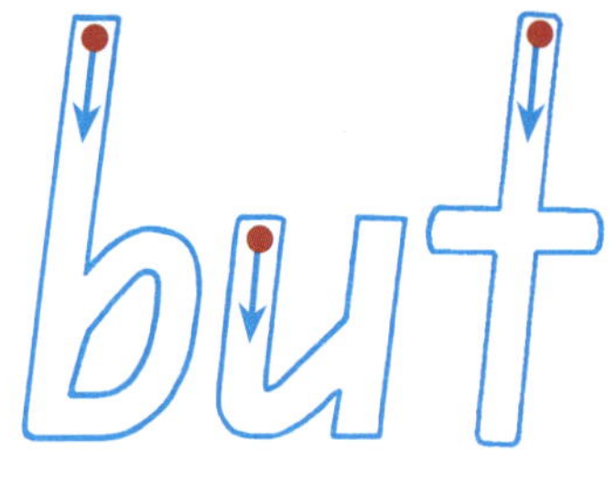

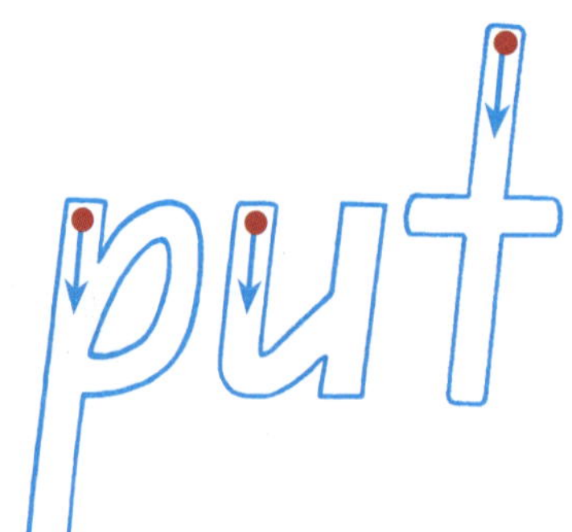

got

2 Colour but = blue, colour put = pink, colour got = green.

3 Complete.

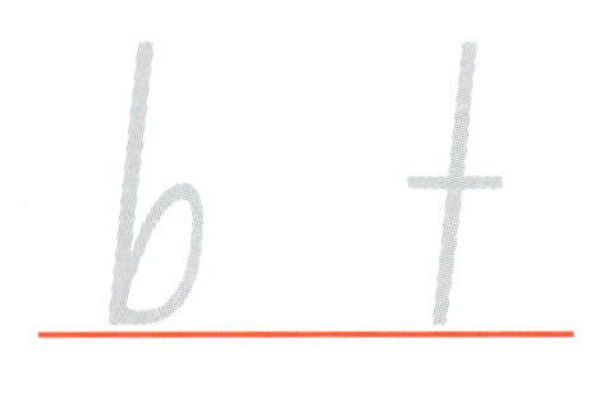

g

4 **Guess the word by its shape. Write each word in a box.**

but put got

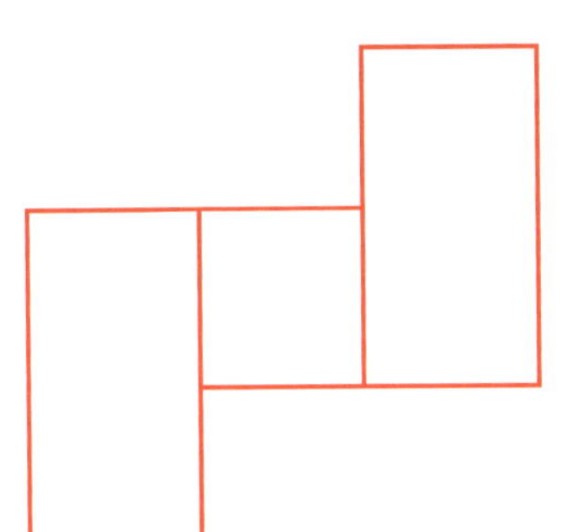

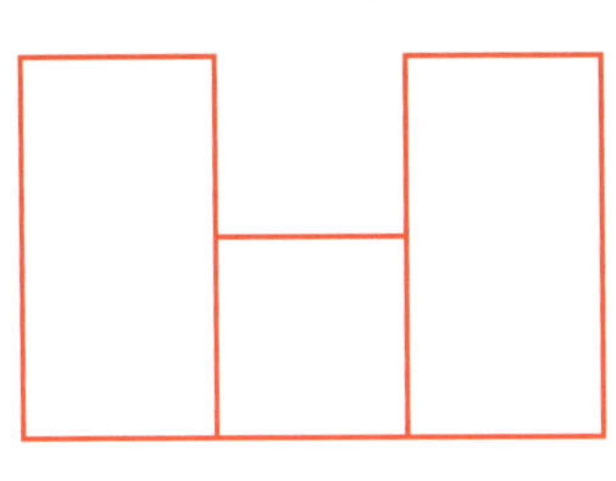

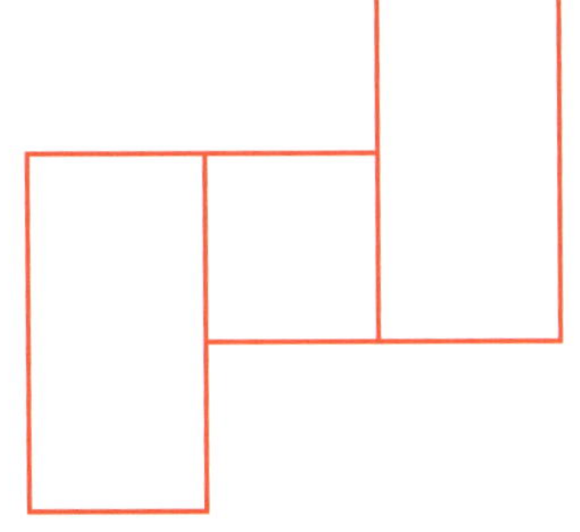

5 **Circle the correct word. Cross out the wrong word.**

Put But your rubbish in the bin.

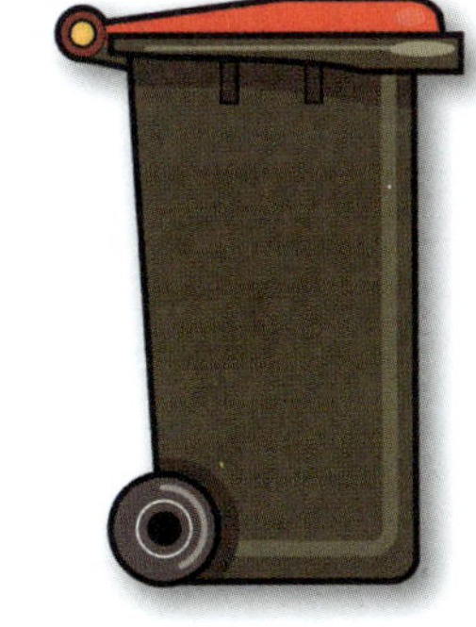

I have put got a puppy.

Shoe Sheep wears shoes but put not socks.

CHALLENGE Circle the hidden words.

abutggotflputbbutngotvput

Lesson 8 • how, now, were

1 Find the matching words.

how	now	were
now	were	how
were	how	now

2 Help Tick Tock Clock find his watch. Colour the path of now words.

now	now	go	low
so	now	now	row
how	on	now	to
cow	bow	now	now

3 Complete the words.

h_w   ___ow   ___ere

4 **Answer the questions.**

How many?	**How** big?	**How** old?

________	________	________

5 **Circle the words.**

How Now Were

How are you Icy Mice? Were you playing in the snow? Now you can make a snowman. How big can you make it?

Colour a snowball each time you find a word.

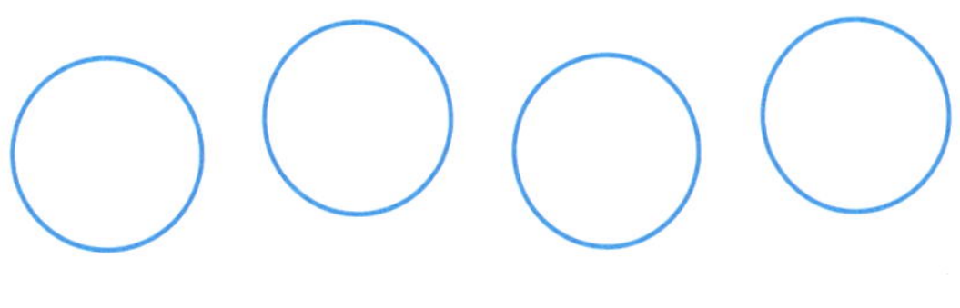

CHALLENGE

Find a rhyming word from your list for:

cow wow her

Fun spot 1

1 **Join each word to a picture that rhymes.**

go

me

too

and

can

got

how

no

2 **Write the words in the correct box.**

we any
the do
to put

2 letter words

3 letter words

Find the words. Colour: so = pink, be = blue, was = yellow, were = red, but = green, he = orange

s	o	w	a	s	w	e	r	e	h	e
b	u	t	w	e	r	e	b	e	s	o
h	e	w	e	r	e	b	e	w	a	s
s	o	b	e	b	u	t	w	e	r	e
w	a	s	h	e	w	e	r	e	s	o
b	e	w	e	r	e	s	o	b	u	t
w	a	s	w	e	r	e	s	o	b	e
h	e	b	e	w	e	r	e	b	u	t
w	a	s	s	o	h	e	w	e	r	e
w	e	r	e	b	u	t	h	e	b	e
w	a	s	h	e	w	e	r	e	s	o
b	e	w	e	r	e	b	u	t	h	e

Lesson 9 • see, saw, say

1 Colour see = green, colour saw = red, colour say = yellow.

2 Join the letters. Write the words.

see saw say

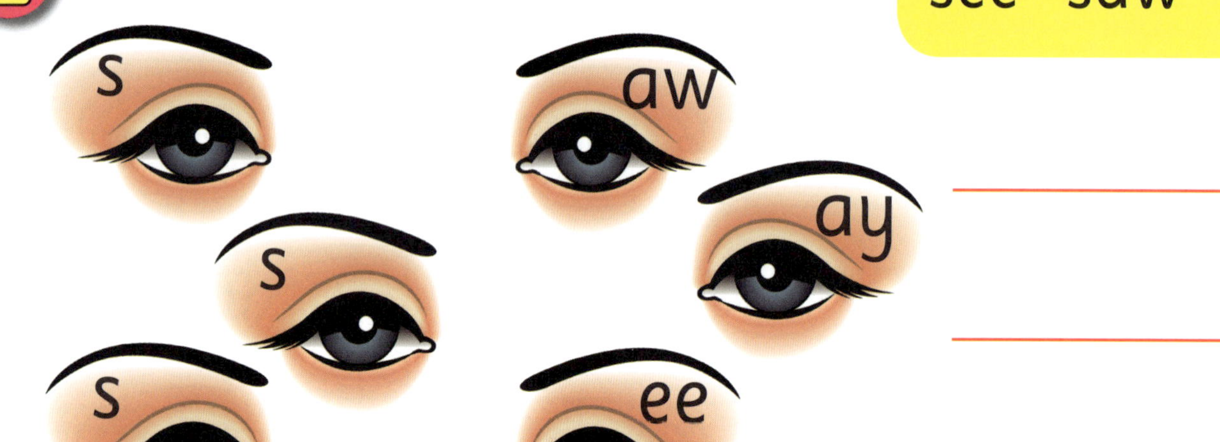

______

______

______

3 Join the words to a picture.

see

say

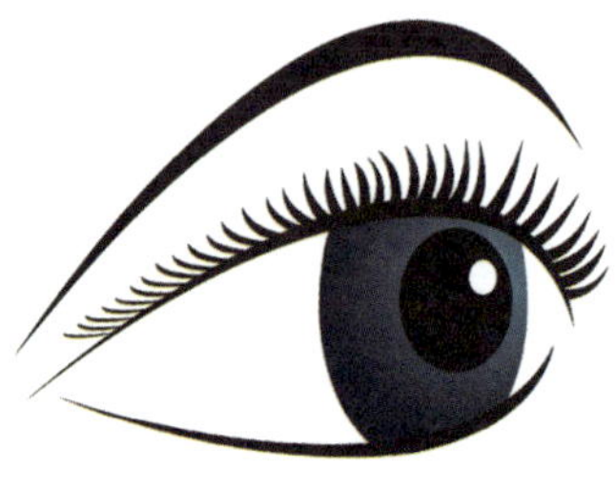

4 Crack the code!

s = ✿
e = ★
a = ✓
y = ■
w = ●

1 ✿ ★ ★ ______

2 ✿ ✓ ■ ______

3 ✿ ✓ ● ______

4 ● ✓ ✿ ______

5 ✓ ✿ ______

6 ■ ★ ✿ ______

5 Complete the sentences.

Say see saw

Did you ______ Flobby today?

I ______ Me Be Fish yesterday.

______ hello to Sid the Kid.

CHALLENGE Write 5 things down that you can see.

Lesson 10 • for, of, not

1 Trace and copy each word.

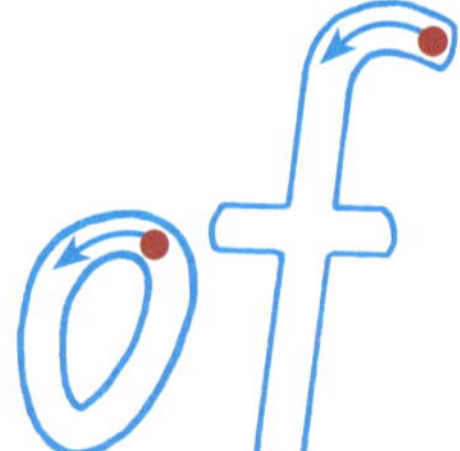

2 Colour the word **for**.

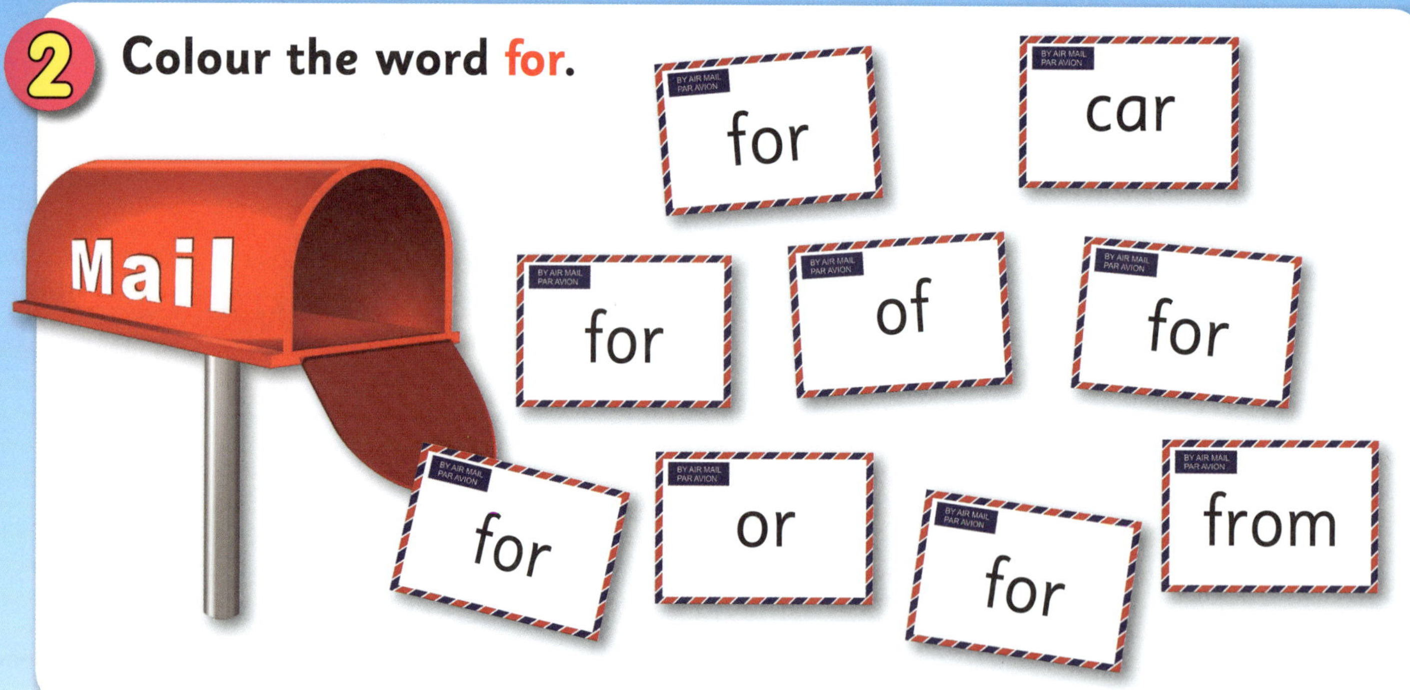

3 Unjumble the words. Write them.

f o

r f o

4 Complete. not

You can  swim.

You can ________ ride.

You can  skate.

5 Circle the correct word. Cross out the wrong word.

I love to eat lots for of cake.

Jake has a gift not for you.

Grumble Goz is of not happy.

I am ready for of bed.

CHALLENGE

Write sentences using these words.

Lesson 11 • his, him, it

1 **Join Dan to the word him.**

him

her

him

him

him

he

him

2 **Complete the labels.** his

his head

eye

ear

tusk

trunk

leg

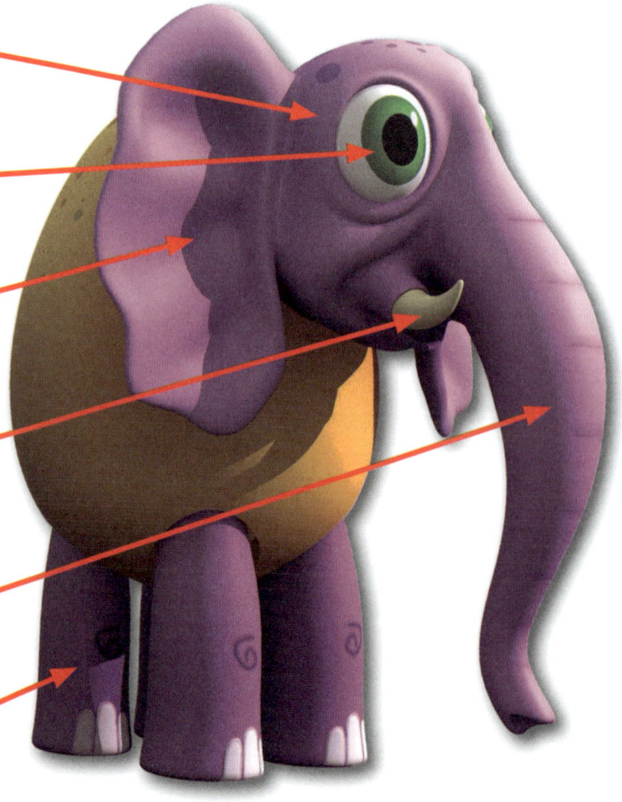

3 Join the words to the pictures.

it

him

4 Guess the word by its shape. Write each word in a box.

his him it

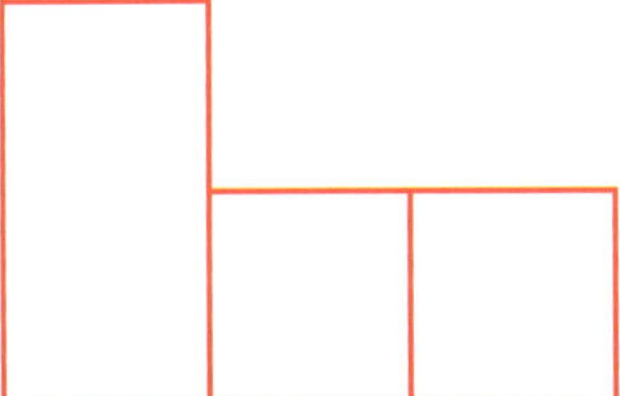
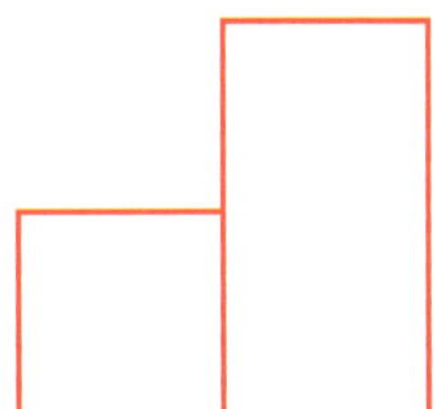
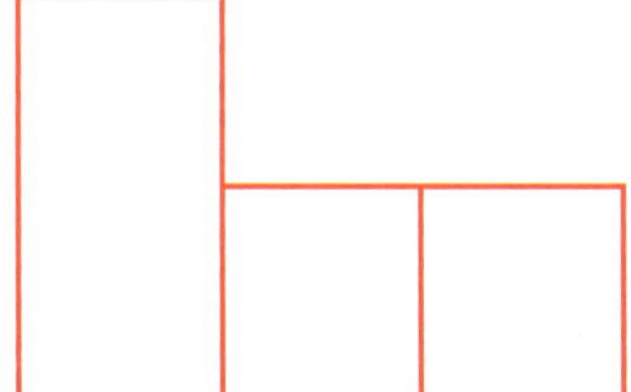

5 Join the words that rhyme.

his	swim
him	lit
it	fizz

CHALLENGE Circle the hidden words.

whiszhimvitnhisohimmit

Lesson 12 • you, your, our

1 Find the matching words.

you	our	your
your	you	our
our	your	you

2 Help Ayee I Owe You to get his money. Colour the path of you words.

you you out yes

our you you your

over you you yell

your our you you

3 Complete the words.

y____ ___our ____ur

4 Read the clue. Write the word.

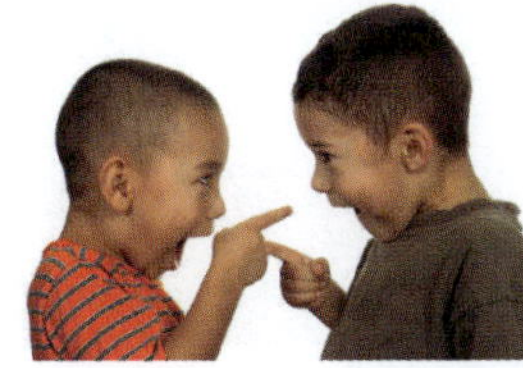

Belonging to you. ____________

Belonging to us. ____________

5 Complete the sentences.

your our you

Can ____________ see Rocky Robot?

Is this ____________ sock, Socky Fox?

Fluff the Duck swims in ____________ pond.

Can ____________ give me a ride, Tug Boat Bug?

CHALLENGE Look for the words

you your our

in an old magazine or newspaper.
Cut them out and glue them on paper.
Write a sentence for each word.

Lesson 13 • are, more, from

1 Colour are = red, colour more = blue, colour from = green.

2 Trace and copy each word.

3 Circle the matching words in each row.

are	our	are	ate
more	move	mare	more
from	form	from	farm

4 **Help Bee Bee Bear to get more honey. Draw a track of are more from words.**

5 **Circle the words.**

Are more from

Are you there, Smile? I have a letter from Meg the Hen. She has got more eggs for you.

Colour a letter each time you find a word.

CHALLENGE

Write a letter to Smile the Crocodile from Meg the Hen.

Lesson 14 • one, only, on

1 Draw.

Only one eye on
Slip and Slide.

Blue Wing sitting
on her nest.

2 Guess the word by its shape. Write each word in a box.

one only on

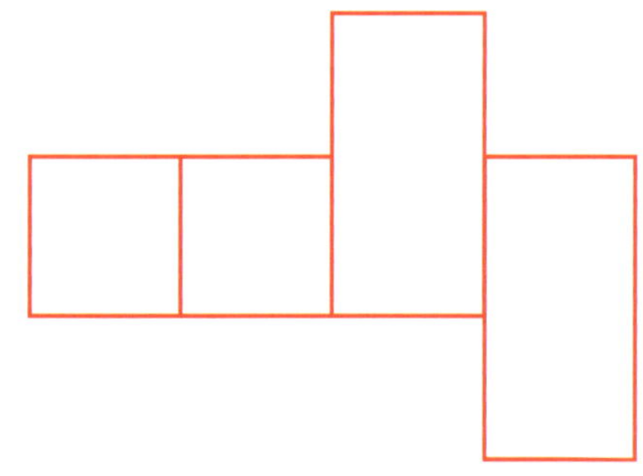

3 Complete the words.

_____n on_____ on_____

4 Crack the code!

o = ▲
n = ●
e = ★
l = ■
y = ✓
s = ✿

1 ▲ ●

____

2 ▲ ● ★

____

3 ▲ ● ■ ✓

____

4 ● ▲

____

5 ✓ ★ ✿

____

6 ✿ ▲

____

5 Circle the words.

one only on

Zeewee plays on the swings. He is funny!
He has only got one tooth and one eye.

Colour a tooth each time you find a word.

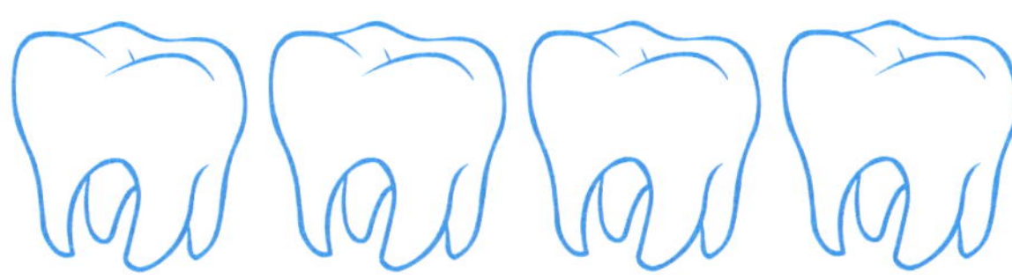

CHALLENGE

Write sentences using the words.

one only on

Lesson 15 • in, into, until

1 Join Insillysect to the word into.

2 Trace and copy each word.

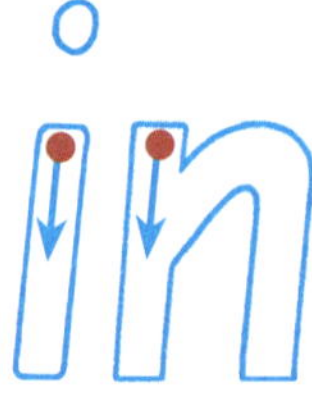

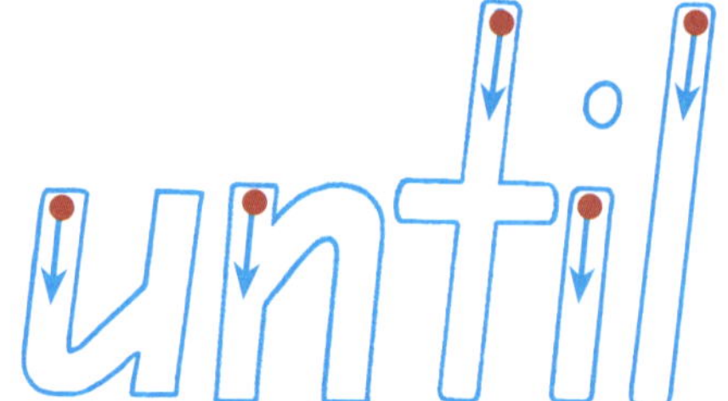

3 Circle the word into.

Pram Lamb got into her pram.

Fluff the Duck got into her bath.

4 Colour yes or no.

Where is Big Pig?

Is he **in** the sea?	yes	no
Is he **in** the park?	yes	no
Is he **in** bed?	yes	no
Is he **in** some mud?	yes	no

5 Circle the correct word. Cross out the wrong word.

You can not eat the cake into until it is ready.

Jump until into the bath!

Wait there in until it is time to go.

Lots of fish swim in until the sea.

CHALLENGE Circle the hidden words.

cinvintogluntilwrinfinto

1 Trace and copy each word.

my why by

2 Find the matching words.

my	why	by
why	by	my
by	my	why

3 Complete.

m___ wh___ ___y

4 Label Nutty Newt's things.

my

This is ________ scarf.

This is ________ hat.

This is ________ sock.

This is ________ bag.

This is ________ shoe.

5 Complete the sentences.

my Why by

________ are you sad, Alphapet?

Gemma Giraffe has got ________ hat.

Frogfish sits ________ the river.

Ding Bat sleeps in ________ tree.

CHALLENGE

Write 4 questions that start with Why.
Remember to put a ? at the end.

Fun spot 2

1 Join the matching words.

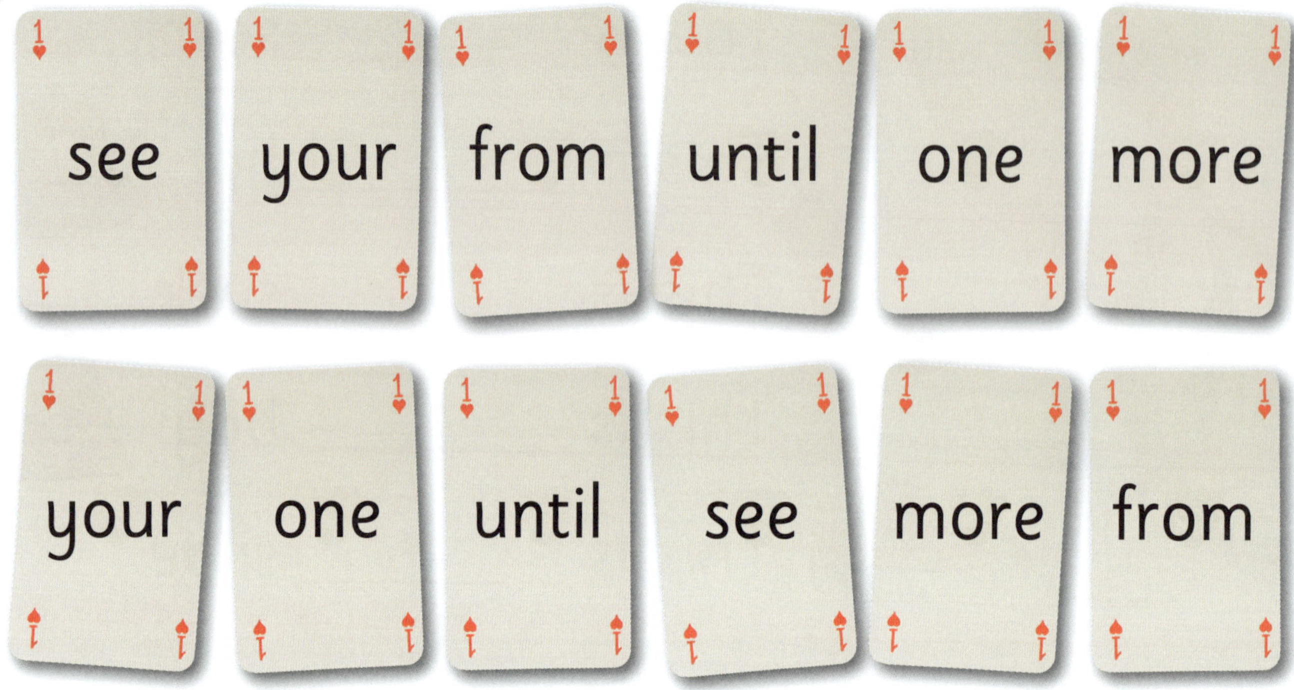

2 Colour 2-letter words = red, 3-letter words = yellow and 4-letter words = green.

3 **Power words. Join the words that rhyme.**

see	more
my	rut
got	now
how	do
to	by
but	me
go	not
your	no

Lesson 17 • her, after, other

1 Help Airy Fairy find her wand. Colour the path of **her** words.

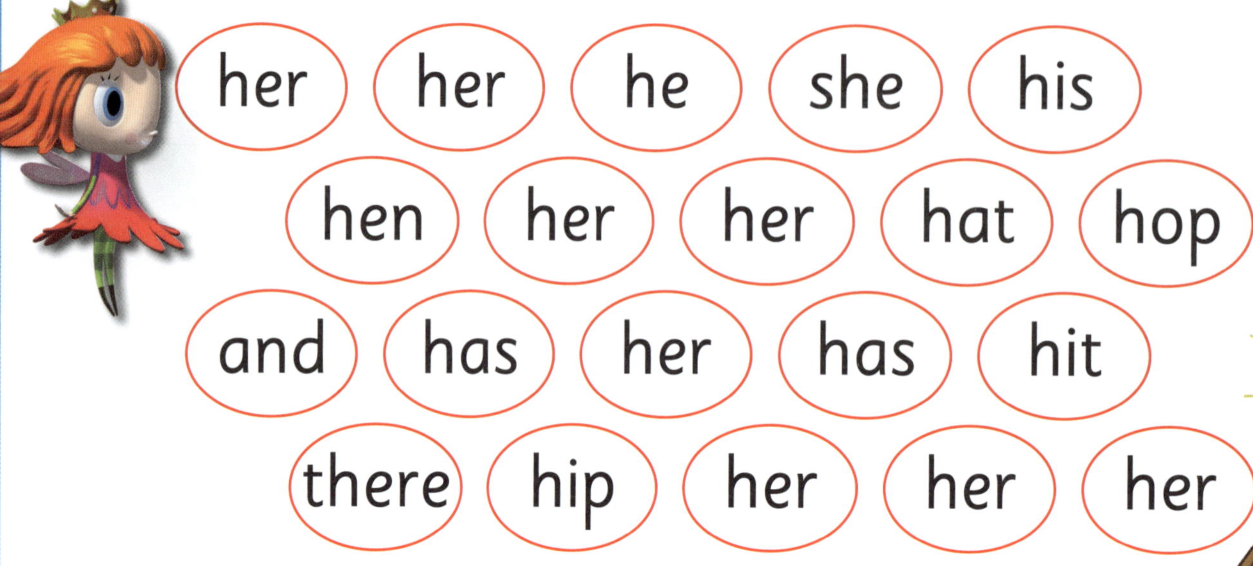

2 Colour the answers.

What comes **after**  ?

What comes **after**  ?

What comes **after**  ?

3 **Guess the word by its shape. Write each word in a box.**

her after other

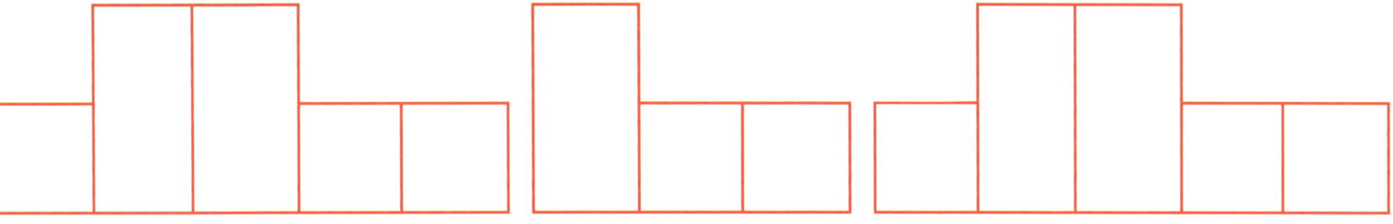

4 **Write each word in alphabetical order.**

other after her

______ ______ ______

5 **Circle the correct word. Cross out the wrong word.**

Shoe Sheep loves after her new shoes.

Socky Fox likes his her other socks best of all.

Tom the Dog will play after other he has had a bone.

CHALLENGE

How many words can you make from the letters **o t h e r**. (You can only use each letter once.)

2 good! 3 great!! +4 WOW!!!

Lesson 18 • with, this, that

1 Colour **with** = **blue**, colour **this** = **red**, colour **that** = **green**.

with this that with

that with this that

2 Circle the matching words in each row.

with	what	when	with
this	those	this	the
that	than	thin	that

3 Trace and copy each word.

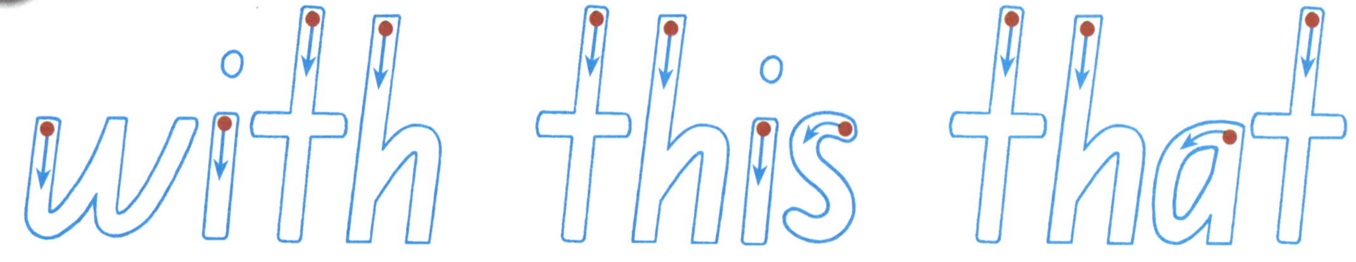

4 **Make words with these letters.**

h a t t

2-letter word:

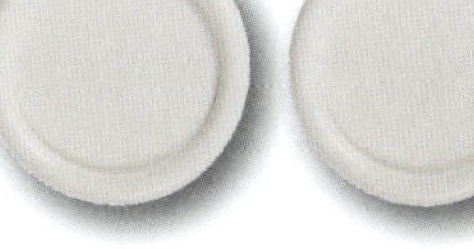

3-letter word:

4-letter word:

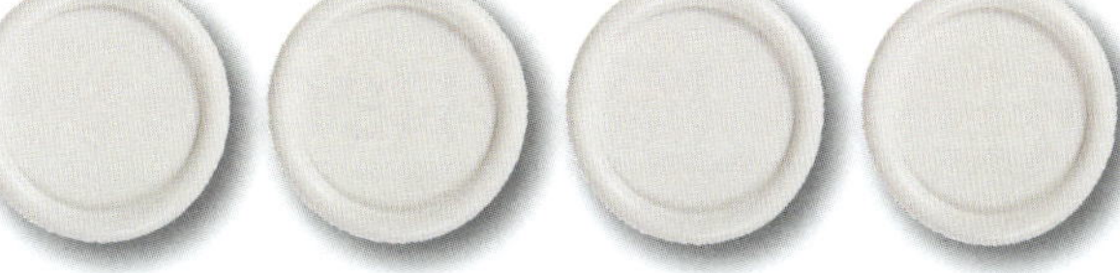

5 **Circle the words.**

with This that

This is Lollipop Mop, and that is Thistle. They are going to the shops with Shelley. This is going to be fun!

Colour a star each time you find a word.

CHALLENGE Look for the words

with this that

in an old magazine or newspaper.
Cut them out and glue them on paper.
Write a sentence for each word.

Lesson 19 • here, where, there

1 Join the word to a picture that rhymes.

where here there

2 Colour there = red, colour where = blue, colour here = green.

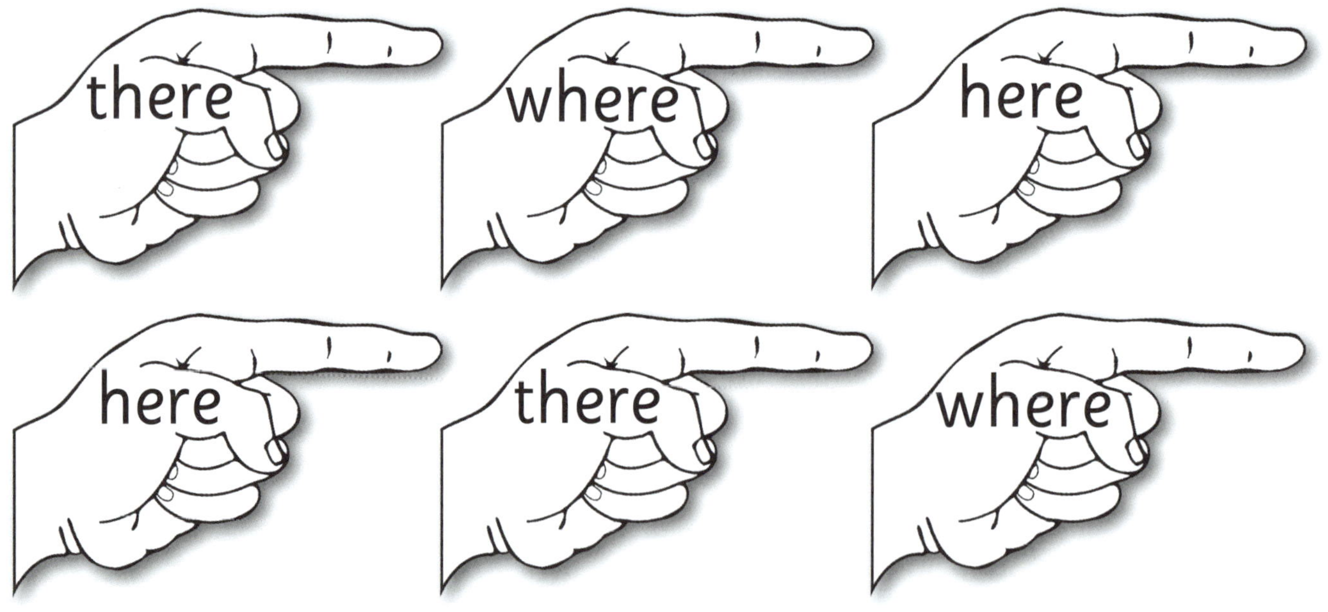

3 Complete the words.

h______ th______ wh______

4 **Help Flutter Bye Bye fly from here to there. Draw a track of here there where words.**

5 **Complete the sentences.**

Here there Where

__________ are you, Octo Puss?

__________ you are!

Let's play over __________.

CHALLENGE

Write 4 questions that start with Where.
Remember to put a ? at the end.

Lesson 20 • then, when, what

1 Circle the word hen in these words:

then when

Circle the word hat in this word:

what

2 Colour when = red, colour what = green.

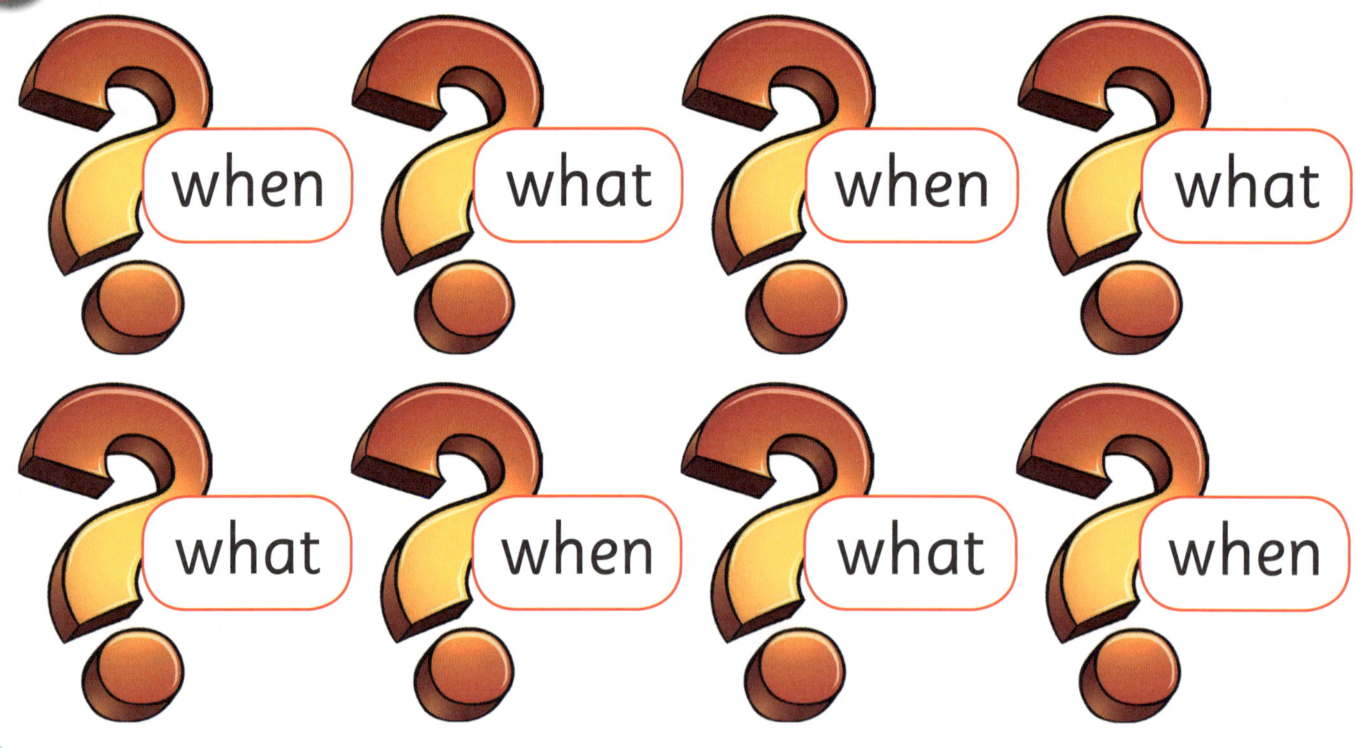

3 Complete the words.

4 Crack the code!

t = ✿
h = ★
e = ■
n = ●
w = ✓
a = ▲

1 ✓ ★ ■ ● ____________

2 ✓ ★ ▲ ✿ ____________

3 ✿ ★ ■ ● ____________

4 ✿ ★ ■ ____________

5 ★ ■ ____________

6 ✓ ■ ● ✿ ____________

5 Circle the correct word. Cross out the wrong word.

When What are you doing, Pinkipoo?

What When can I have a ride on your bike?

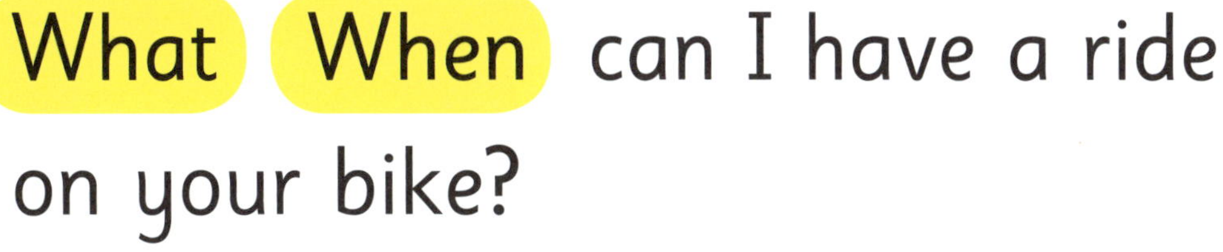

First we will have cake, then what we will have ice-cream. Yum!

CHALLENGE

Write 4 questions that start with What and When.
Remember to put a ? at the end.

Lesson 21 • than, these, thing

1 Join Thingamabob to the word thing.

2 Complete the sentences. than

Octo Puss is bigger ________ Underting.

Eggyphant is bigger ________ Octo Puss.

Underting is smaller ________ Eggyphant.

3 Make words with these letters.

e t e s h

2-letter word: 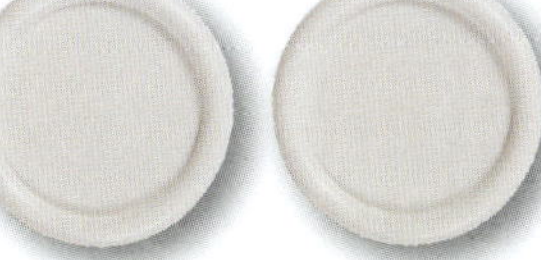

3-letter word: 

5-letter word: 

4 Complete the sentences.

than these thing

Are ____________ your socks, Socky Fox?

Are you bigger ____________ Jazz the Cat?

This ____________ belongs to Go Go Gizmo and ____________ carrots must be Red Rabbit's.

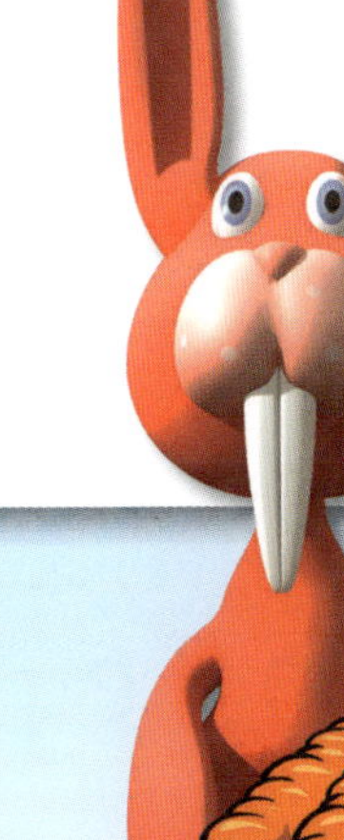

CHALLENGE

Write sentences using these words.

than these thing

Lesson 22 • they, them, their

1 Join the word to a picture that rhymes.

they

them

their

2 Trace and copy each word.

them

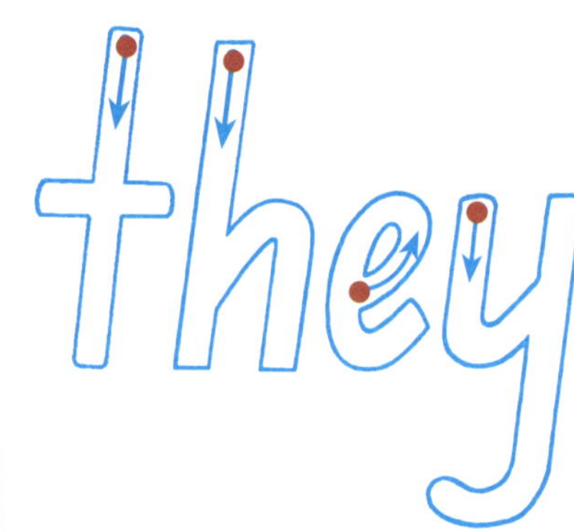

3 Join the letters. Write the words

th ey

th em

th eir

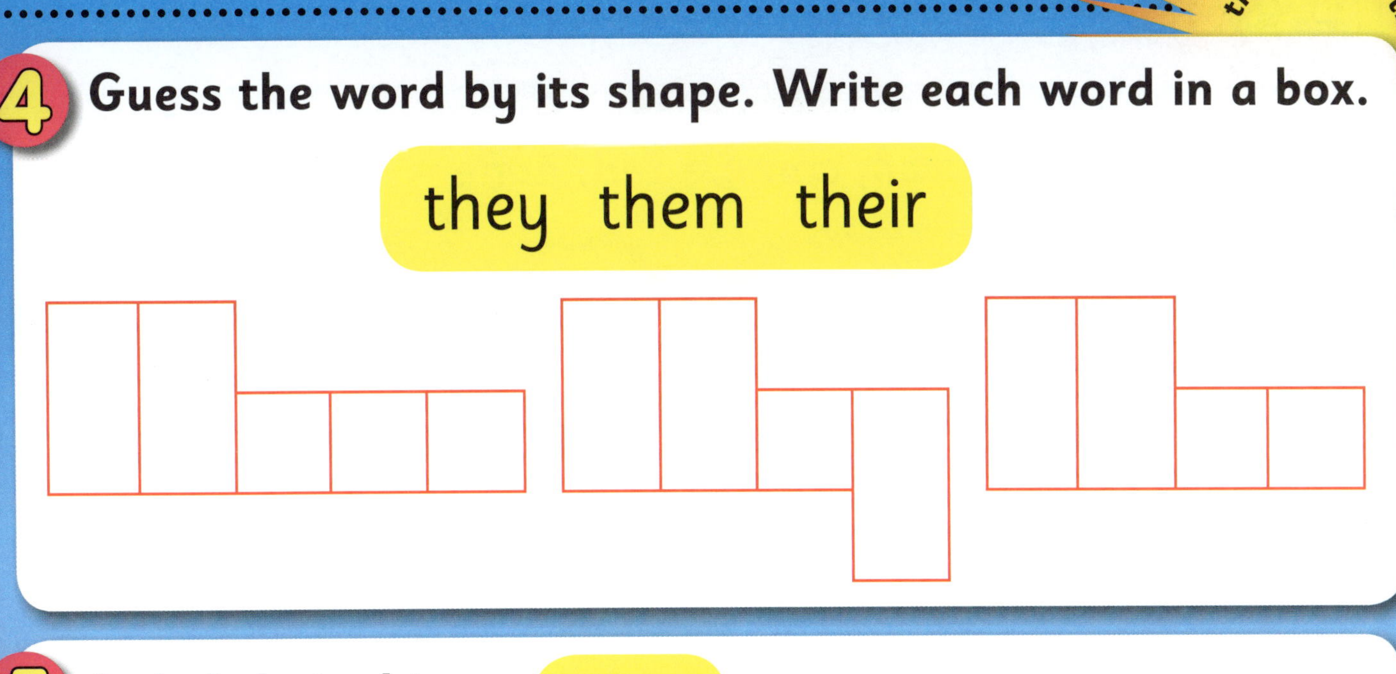

4 Guess the word by its shape. Write each word in a box.

they them their

5 Label their things.

their

______ gloves

______ socks

______ boots

______ hats

______ scarves

6 Circle the words.

They them their

This is Tom and Dogfin. I play with them at their house. They are funny.

Colour a bone each time you find a word.

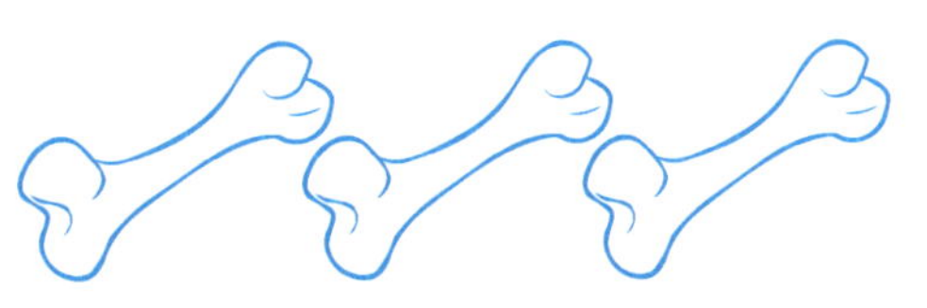

Lesson 23 • some, come, done

1 Colour some = green, come = red, done = blue.

some come done come some done

2 Circle the matching words in each row.

some	so	same	some
come	came	cone	come
done	don't	done	does

3 Guess the word by its shape. Write each word in a box.

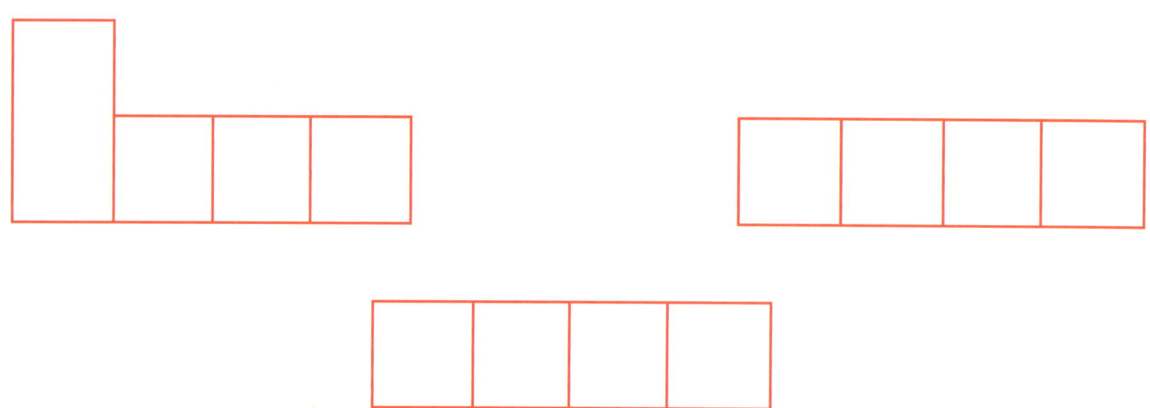

4 Help Shoe Sheep to find some shoes. Draw a track of **some come done** words.

5 Complete the sentences.

done some come

Bee Bee Bear has __________ honey for me.

Can Baby Face __________ to my party?

Have you __________ all of your jobs, Lollipop Mop?

CHALLENGE

Write down 3 things that you have done today.

I have done . . .

Lesson 24 • give, have, leave

1 Join the pieces. Write the words.

____

____

____

2 Colour yes or no.

I **have** one eye.	yes	no
I **have** ten legs.	yes	no
I **have** one tooth.	yes	no
I **have** blue hair.	yes	no

3 Complete the words.

giv___ ___ave lea___e

4 Follow the instructions.

Give Marshmallow Mouse a big, pink hat.

Give Smile the Crocodile an apple pie.

5 Circle the correct word. Cross out the wrong word.

Please have give me that ball.

What time does your train leave give ?

I leave have not washed my hands.

CHALLENGE

Write these words in alphabetical order.

leave give have

Choose one word to write in a sentence.

Fun spot 3

1 **Colour: her = red, with = green, here = yellow, then = pink, they = orange, some = blue, give = purple, after = brown, this = black**

2 Write the words in the correct cloud.

there these
when them
other that

4-letter words

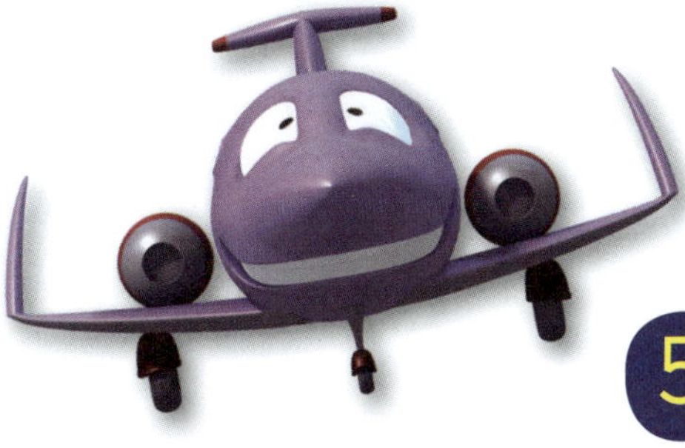

5-letter words

3 Join the matching words.

come	their	leave	thing	have	what
leave	have	thing	what	come	their

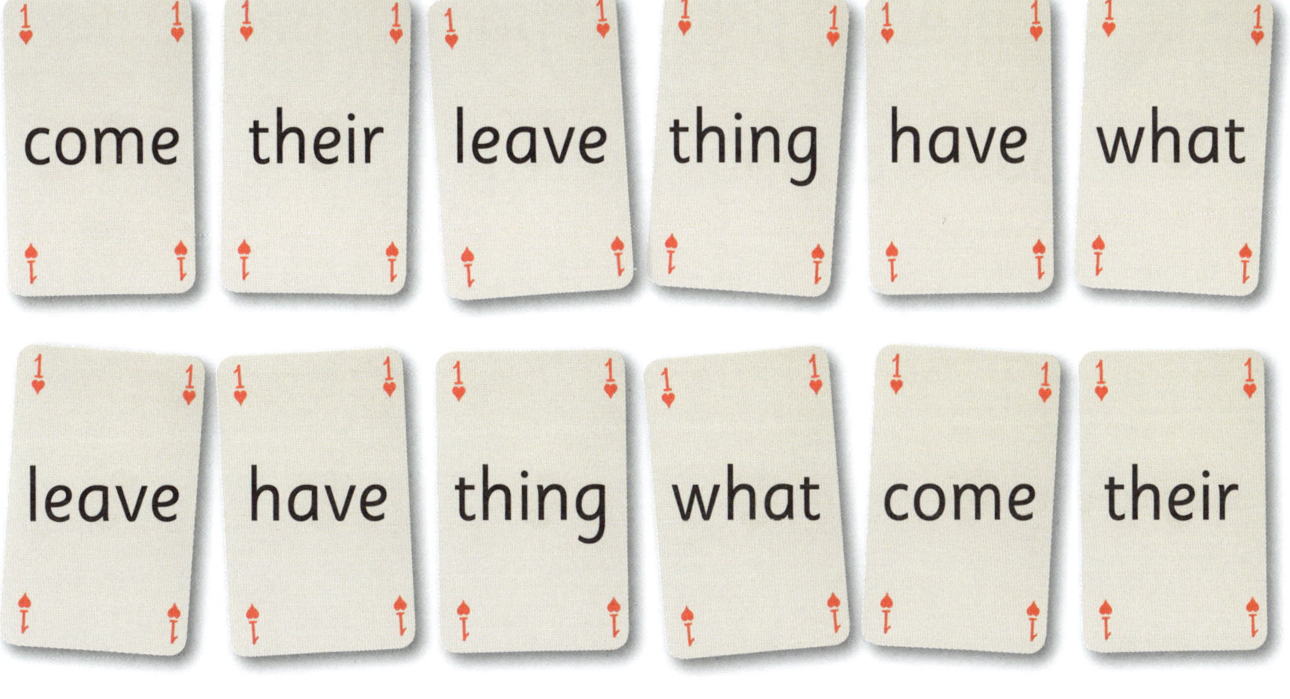

Lesson 25 • little, better, pretty

1 Trace and copy each word.

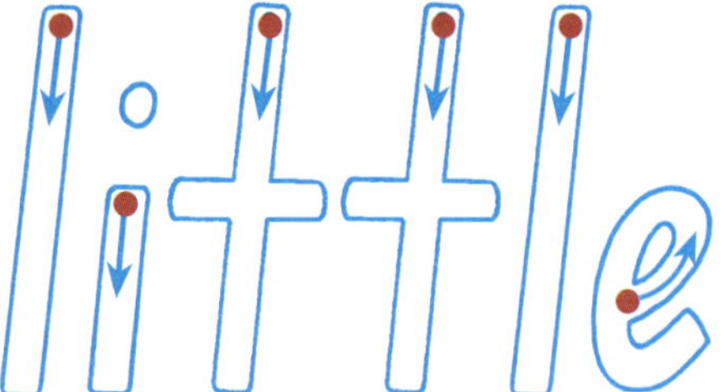

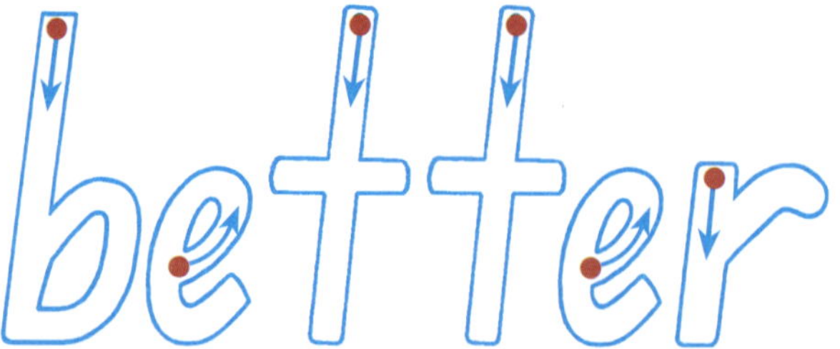

2 Help Issy Me to get to the pretty flowers. Colour the path of pretty words.

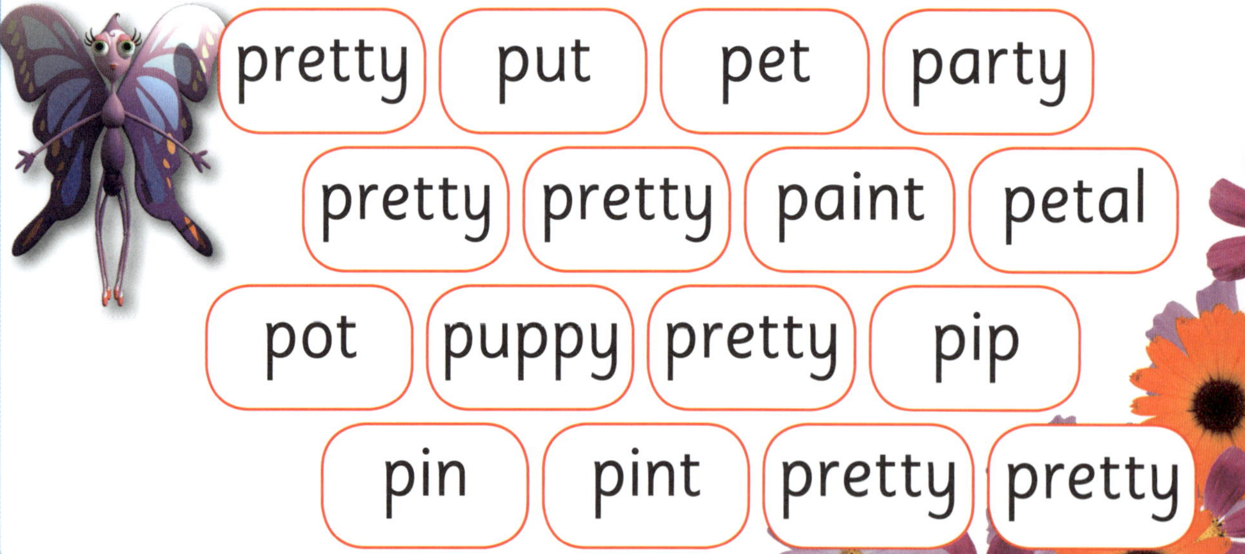

3 Complete the words.

pre__y be__er li__le

4 **Draw:**

a pretty bunch of flowers for Dotty Sun Spot.

a little bone for Gutter Mutt.

5 **Circle the words.**

little better pretty

Poor Wheely Whale. He was feeling a little bit sick. Zen Ten drew him a pretty picture. That made Wheely Whale feel much better.

Colour a picture each time you find a word.

CHALLENGE

Find a word in your list that means the same as:

small lovely not sick

Lesson 26 • which, who, while

1 Join the word to a picture that rhymes.

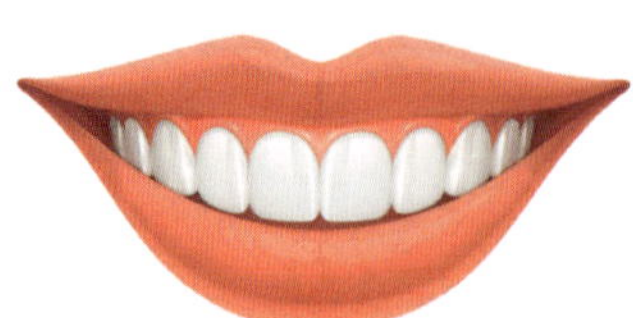

which

who

while

2 Complete.

Sunny Snail

Octo Puss

Xpanda

Who has eight legs? ____________________

Who is black and white? ____________________

Who has a shell? ____________________

3 Complete the words.

wh__________ ______ich ______o

4 Crack the code!

w =
h =
i =
l =
e =
o =
c =
n =

1 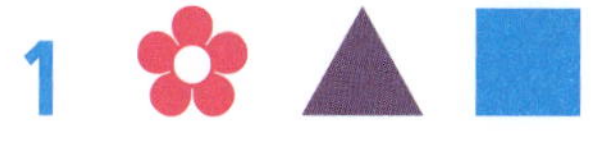

____

2 

____

3

____

4 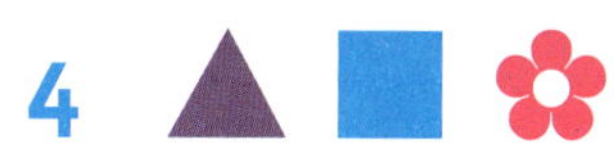

____

5

____

6

____

5 Circle the correct word. Cross out the wrong word.

Wait a while which before you go swimming, Frogfish.

While Who does this hat belong to?

Which While pencil is mine?

CHALLENGE

Write sentences using these words.

who which while

Lesson 27 • could, would, should

1 Join the pieces. Write the words.

2 Colour could = pink, colour would = blue, colour should = green.

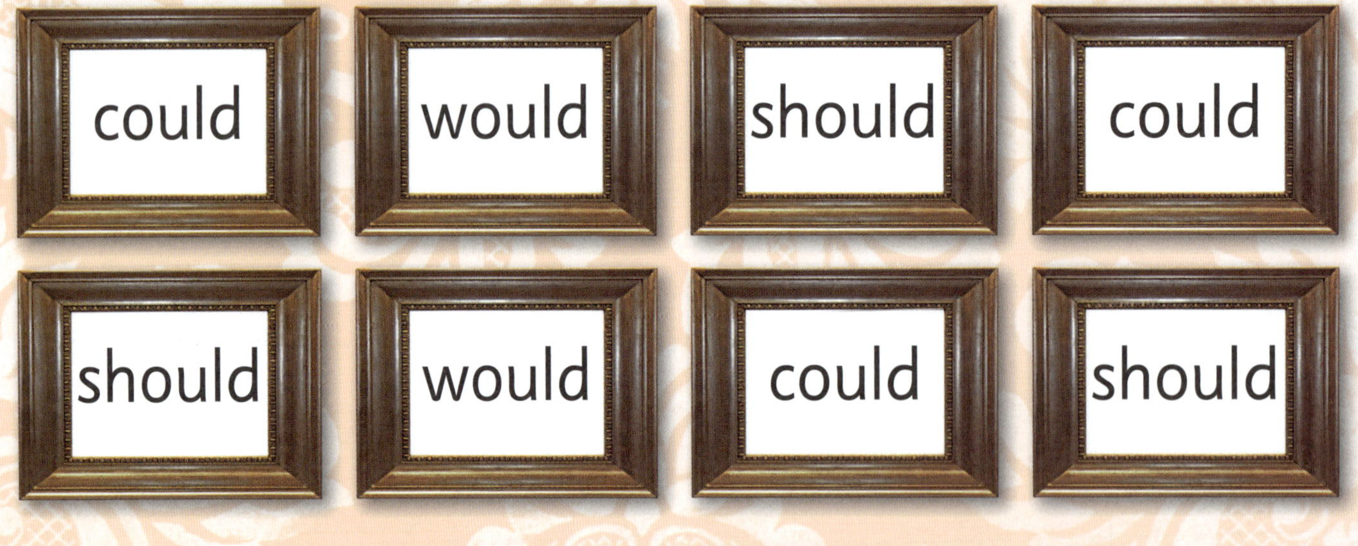

3 Complete the words.

coul______ shou______ w______d

4

Draw a picture of yourself here.

Answer yes or no.

Could you eat 10 ice-creams?	yes	no
Should you brush your teeth?	yes	no
Would you like to fly to the moon?	yes	no

5 **Complete the sentences.**

could Would should

________ you like to play with Buzzle Top?

You ________ tell a grown up before you go out.

I ________ run faster than Dan.

CHALLENGE

Write these words in alphabetical order.

would could should

Lesson 28 • said, again, pair

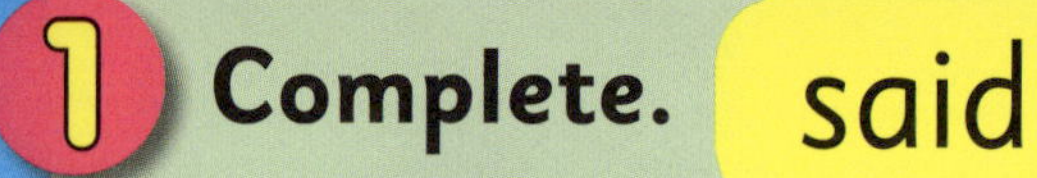

1 Complete. said

"I can tell the time," ________ Tick Tock Clock.

"I have a lot of spines," ________ Hedgehog Dog.

"Zoom, zoom! I can go very fast," ________ Eggster.

2 Find the matching pairs.

3 **Help Socky Fox to find his pair of socks. Draw a track of said again pair words.**

4 **Circle the words.** said again pair

"Hello!" said Yabby Dabby Do. "I have a pair of big claws. SNAP! SNAP!" Yabby, can you snap your claws again?

Colour a picture each time you find a word.

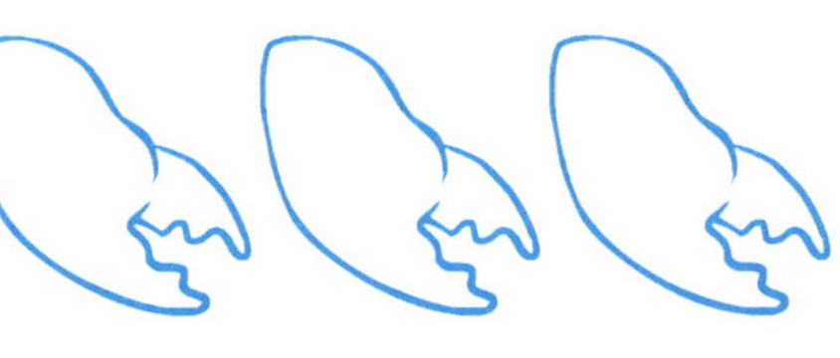

CHALLENGE Circle the hidden words.

esaidfgagainvwpairdnagain

Lesson 29 • about, out, house

1 Join Wrecking Ball to the word house.

house

has

mouse

house

hose

his

house

2 Trace and copy each word.

house about

3 Colour the word out.

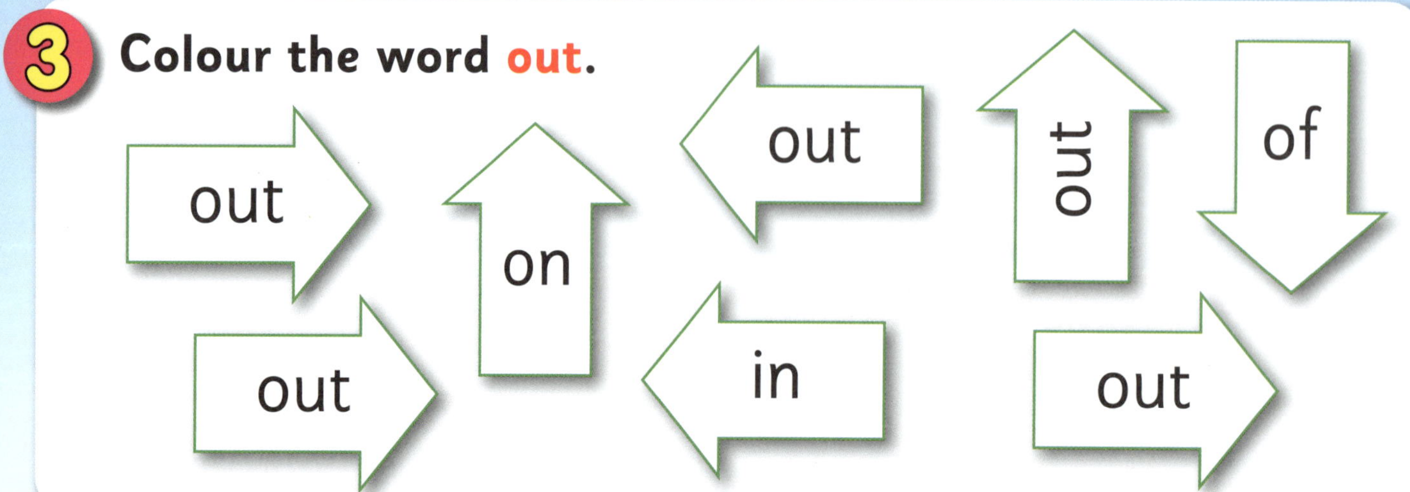

4 Complete.

Colour the book about dogs = blue.
Colour the book about fish = orange.
Colour the book about cats = green.
Colour the book about birds = red.

5 Circle the correct word. Cross out the wrong word.

Alphapet read a story out about rabbits.

Can we play at your house out today?

Let's go house out to the park.

CHALLENGE

Write 3 sentences about your house.

Lesson 30 • all, shall, will

1 Colour all = yellow, colour shall = pink, colour will = blue.

2 Guess the word by its shape. Write each word in a box.

all shall will

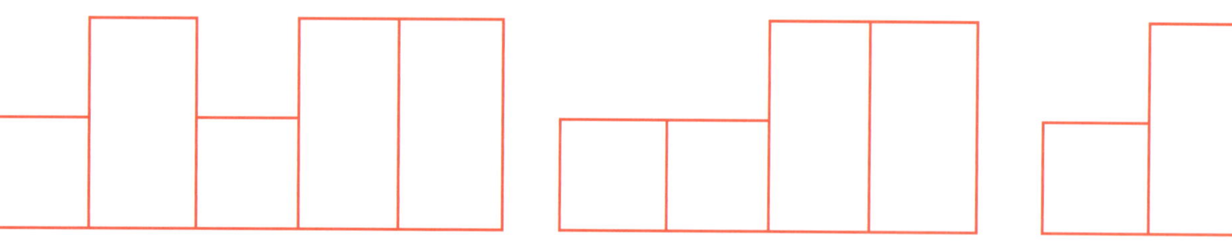

3 Circle the matching words in each row.

all	and	all	are
shall	she	shell	shall
will	we	will	wall

4 **Help Red Rabbit to find all his carrots. Colour the path of all words.**

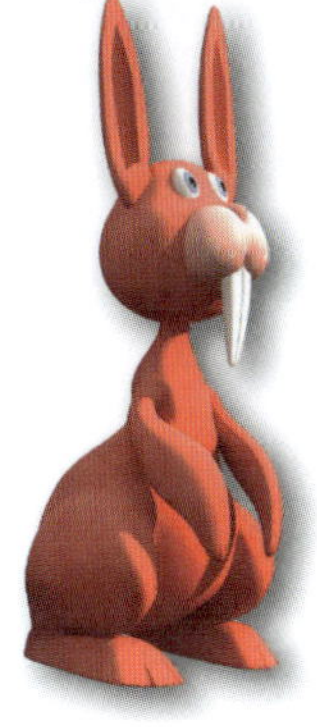

all	all	bell	ball	fall
fall	all	ill	hill	tell
call	all	wall	sell	full
mill	all	all	all	all

5 **Complete the sentences.**

all will Shall

Have you eaten __________ of the cake, Catty Cake?

__________ I close the window?

Big Pig, __________ you play with me?

CHALLENGE

Write these words in alphabetical order.

will all shall

Choose one word to write in a sentence.

Lesson 31 • because, before, been

1. Trace and copy each word.

before been

2. Guess the word by its shape. Write each word in a box.

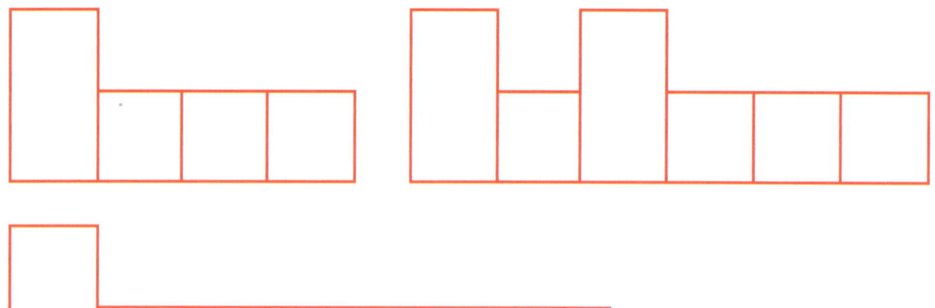

because
before
been

3. Colour the answers.

What comes before  ?

What comes before ?

What comes before  ?

What comes before ?

4 **Complete.**

because

Wobble Blob was not very hungry

__________ he ate 5 ice-creams.

__________ he ate too much jelly.

__________ he ate a box of popcorn.

5 **Circle the words.**

because before been

Where have you been, Gemma? We must go and visit Peggy Leg before it gets too late. Bring your hat because it is very sunny.

Colour a hat each time you find a word.

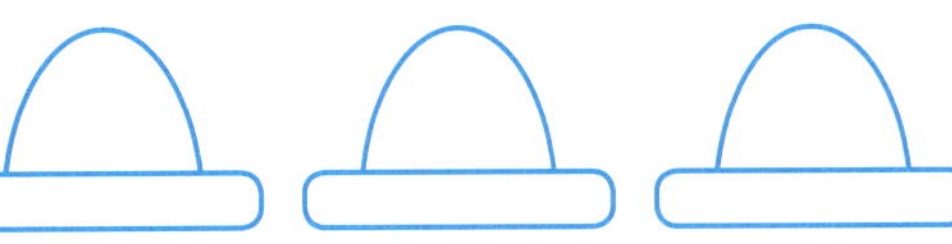

CHALLENGE

Write 4 reasons for not wanting to go to bed. Start each sentence with: I don't want to go to bed **because** ...

Lesson 32 • also, always, along

1 Colour also = blue, colour always = yellow, colour along = green.

2 Complete the sentences. also

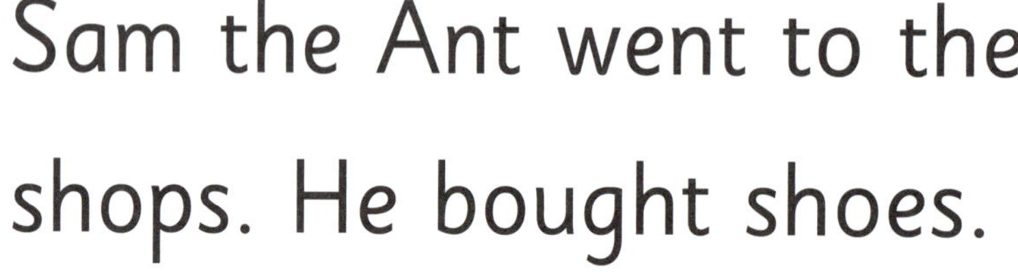

Sam the Ant went to the shops. He bought shoes.

He ______________ bought a hat.

He ______________ bought a coat.

He ______________ bought a bag.

He ______________ bought a scarf.

3 Make words with these letters.

1-letter word:

3-letter word:

4-letter word:

6-letter word:

4 Complete the sentences.

also always along

Smile loves pies. He __________ likes to wear ties.

Tug Boat Bug sails __________ the river.

You are __________ sleepy, Happy Nap.

Airy Fairy can fly. She can __________ skip and jump.

CHALLENGE

How many words can you make from the letters along. (You can only use each letter once.)

3 - good! 4 - great! + 5 - WOW!

Fun spot 4

1 Join each word to a picture that rhymes.

pair

who

said

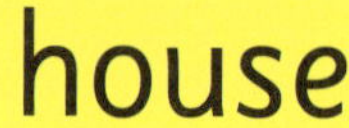

house

while

been

all

2 Write the words in the correct box.

pretty better
shall should
again about

5-letter words

6-letter words

3 Find the words. Colour: along = red, would = blue, again = pink, about = orange, house = green, which = yellow

w	h	i	c	h	a	b	o	u	t
a	l	o	n	g	a	g	a	i	n
h	o	u	s	e	w	o	u	l	d
w	h	i	c	h	h	o	u	s	e
a	g	a	i	n	w	o	u	l	d
a	l	o	n	g	a	b	o	u	t
w	h	i	c	h	h	o	u	s	e
w	o	u	l	d	a	l	o	n	g
h	o	u	s	e	a	g	a	i	n
a	b	o	u	t	w	o	u	l	d
a	g	a	i	n	w	h	i	c	h
a	l	o	n	g	h	o	u	s	e

ABC
Reading
eggs
AMAZING!
You know your
sight words!